GETTING TO KNOW
JESUS

PAUL
STEEVES

InterVarsity Press
Downers Grove, Illinois 60515

Bible quotations are
taken from the following:
King James Version (KJV),
New English Bible (NEB),
J. B. Phillips, "The New
Testament in Modern English"
(Phillips) and Revised Standard
Version (RSV)

Third printing under
the present title, January
1975. Originally issued
under the title "The Character
and Work of Jesus Christ."
Revised edition © 1967
by Inter-Varsity Christian
Fellowship of the
United States of America.
InterVarsity Press
is the book publishing
division of Inter-Varsity
Christian Fellowship.

ISBN 0-87784-663-4
Library of Congress
Catalog Card
Number: 67-28019

Printed in the
United States of America

TABLE OF CONTENTS

SUGGESTED LECTURE TOPICS AND DISCUSSION PASSAGES

A The Claims of Jesus Christ and the Reliability
of New Testament Documents, John 8:31-59
B Jesus' Claims on Us, Luke 9:23-27, 57-62; 14:25-35
C The Love of the Lord Jesus, John 15:1-17
D The Meaning of Jesus' Death, Isaiah 52:13—53:12
E Evidences of the Resurrection, I Corinthians 15:1-28

FOREWORD

PURPOSE
This series has two aims:
1. to increase your understanding of Jesus Christ, who He is, and what He has done ,and
2. to help you discover how this understanding is relevant to daily life in order that you may live a consistent Christian life.

The Bible studies in this series confront the reader with the dynamic personality of Jesus Christ and open the way for a greater appreciation of Him.

MATERIALS
In addition to this study guide, you will need the following:
1. a Bible,
2. a pen—you increase your retention by being active (writing) in the study, and
3. *Basic Christianity* by John R. W. Stott, the textbook for this series. Frequent reference will be made to this book; if you do not already own a copy, you may purchase one from Inter-Varsity Press for $1.50.

DESIGN
You will need determination and discipline in order to get the most out of these studies. They may be used for either per-

sonal or group study. Group use of this series also includes personal study.

FOR PERSONAL STUDY

The suggested daily study period is thirty minutes. First, read the suggested passage and try to discover its most important features. Then, answer the questions given. It is best to write the answers as this will make them clear in your mind. Third, read the brief comments. Think through the application questions next; this is the step of making the passage relevant to your own life. If time permits or interest motivates you, launch into the suggested further study.

FOR GROUP STUDY

Individuals follow directions for personal study. A twenty-minute lecture followed by several small-group discussions is probably the best organization for the group meeting. The topic is one of the six daily studies. The lecture should be devoted to a presentation of material which is relevant to this topic. The lecture should be a thought-provoker, or a *primer,* that stimulates thinking for the group discussions.

The group discussions provide an opportunity to talk about what each member has been studying during the week. These student-led discussions should concentrate on one of the daily studies, but questions or observations from any of the week's materials will be appropriate.

Students or other individuals meet with the same group for each of the five discussions in this series. With this arrangement a few students will become better acquainted and develop freedom to express themselves. Individual preparation is important; such preparation makes the discussion more beneficial for each participant.

This study series could also be used by dispensing with the lecture and spending a longer period of time in group interaction on the chosen topic.

STUDY **A**

THE DEITY OF JESUS CHRIST

Mark 2:1-12

DAY **1**

a claim to forgive sin (an indirect claim to deity)

QUESTIONS

1. Compare Jesus' attitude toward the sick man and his friends with that of the scribes and Pharisees. *Jesus had Compassion for the sick man -*

2. Did Jesus agree that only God could forgive sins? *no*. What does the healing demonstrate? *His authority doesn't stop at the healing - it includes the forgiving of sins.*

COMMENTS

The claim to forgive sins was, in Jewish culture, a claim to exercise a prerogative that was only God's. Tasker says, "As the scribes were rightly thinking, it is blasphemy for a mere man to claim the authority to forgive, for no human being can with absolute justice assess the motives, and therefore the guilt, of another."[1] Only the offended one can forgive an offense. This occasion is not the only time Jesus claimed power to forgive sin. He amazed the Pharisees in Luke 7:47-50 with a similar incident.

The significance of the miracle is not only that it proves

[1]R. V. G. Tasker, *Commentary on the Gospel According to St. Matthew* (Grand Rapids: Eerdmans Publishing Co., 1961), p. 94. Used by permission.

Jesus can forgive sin, but also that Jesus thought and declared He had power to forgive sins and then validated His claim by a miraculous act. Jesus thus claims for Himself an authority which is God's.

APPLICATION

1. Record here what you learned from this passage about Jesus.

He cares for each of us no matter what your analyzed condition we are in.

2. What confidence can you have in Him as a result of these facts? _He will instruct me thru his words + actions._

FURTHER STUDY

1. Jesus makes other indirect claims to His deity. These include:

   a. the power to give life (John 5:21, John 6:35, John 11:25),

   b. direct access to truth (Mark 6:2, Mark 13:31, John 12:48),

   c. the authority to judge the world (Matthew 25:31-46, John 5:27-29).

2. *Basic Christianity,* pages 29-32.

STUDY **A**

THE DEITY OF JESUS CHRIST

DAY **2**

a direct claim to deity

John 8:31-59

QUESTIONS

1. Note the frequency of reference to truth in this passage.

   a. What will the truth do for someone? *set you free*.

   b. Where did Jesus get the truth He spoke?_____

   _____ .

2. In verses 37-49, what two claims of these people does Jesus refute?_____

   _____

   What reasoning does He use to do so?_____

   _____

3. In verses 48-59, what two comparisons are made between Jesus and Abraham?_____

   _____

4. In this section, what claims does Jesus make about His teaching?_____

   _____

COMMENTS

This passage includes one of the most amazing statements ever made by a man: "Before Abraham was, I am." So amazing was this statement that it incited the Jews to pick up stones to throw at the One who made it. Their Law prescribed the penalty of stoning for the crime of blasphemy; in their zeal they took it upon themselves to carry out that penalty.

But what was the blasphemy? It was in the words, "I am." By tense, these words indicate the eternal existence of the One who said them. "Abraham was" indicates simple past tense; "I am," a condition uniformly the same from the beginning to the end, implies eternity. John said the same in John 1:1, "When all things began, the Word already was" (NEB). More precisely, however, these words are a claim to deity, not simply eternity. Jesus Christ used this expression, "I am," several times. It is significant because through it He clearly applied to Himself a designation which had often been used by God of Himself in the Old Testament. See Exodus 3:14 as an example.

APPLICATION

1. Think about the attributes usually associated with "father." What does it mean to you to know that God is a *Father* to you (v. 42)?_____

_____

2. What outward manifestations in your life come from the fact that God is your Father?_____

_____

FURTHER STUDY

1. Study Moses' encounter with God in Exodus 3:13-15.
2. Study another claim of Jesus to oneness with God which provoked an attempted stoning in John 10:30-33. See also John 5:18.
3. *Basic Christianity,* pages 26-29.

4. *Son of Man, Is Jesus Christ Unique?* by Richard Wolff.
5. "Jesus' View of Himself" in *The Lord from Heaven,* by Leon Morris, pages 26-43.
6. *The Fact of Christ,* by P. Carnegie Simpson.
7. In the third century, an argument raged within the Christian Church as to whether Jesus was "of like substance with the Father," or "of the same substance as the Father." These concepts are translations of the Greek words *homoiousia* and *homoousia* respectively; the difference is just one letter. But the real difference was seen to be enormous. Which of these expressions do you think is most in accord with New Testament teaching? Support your answer. (The remainder of these studies may help you in answering this question.)

STUDY **A**

THE DEITY OF
JESUS CHRIST

John 8:28-47

DAY **3**

Jesus' sinlessness

QUESTIONS

1. What does Jesus say about the effects of sin on a person?

_____

What implies that one is not necessarily aware of this servitude?

_____

2. What indications are there that Jesus thought of Himself as sinless? Why is verse 46 remarkable?_____

_____

_____

3. What did Jesus' followers say in the following passages?

   a. II Corinthians 5:21_____

   b. Hebrews 4:15, 7:26_____

   c. I Peter 2:22_____

   d. I John 3:5 _____

4. What does Jesus' sinlessness contribute to your understanding of who He is?_____

_____

COMMENTS

"The PERFECT holiness of Christ is proved in this passage not by the silence of the Jews, who might very well have ignored the sins of their interlocutor, but by the assurance with which Jesus lays this question (John 8:46) before them."[2] Jesus is calmly confident as He asks this question. He has previously asserted that He always does God's will. He is without sin—a state of perfect obedience. Here is true manhood in its intended relation to God.

APPLICATION

1. In order to be perfect, why is it not enough merely to avoid sin?_____

_____

2. In the light of this passage, why is continual acquaintance with God's Word necessary?_____

_____

3. Of what help is it to you to see Jesus as the example of manhood as God intends man to be?_____

_____

Of what value is a detailed study of His life?_____

_____

FURTHER STUDY

1. *Basic Christianity*, pages 35-45.
2. *Son of Man* (Wolff), pages 29-47.
3. "The Sinlessness of Jesus" in *The Lord from Heaven* (Morris), pages 21-25.

[2]Frederick Godet, *Gospel of John* (Grand Rapids: Zondervan Publishing House, 1956), p. 118. Used by permission.

STUDY **A**

THE DEITY OF
JESUS CHRIST

John 14:1-11

DAY **4**

*Jesus' revelation
of God*

QUESTIONS

1. What claims does Jesus make in this passage

    a. about the relationship between God and man?_____

    _____

    b. about the relationship between God and Himself?_____

    _____

2. Why do you think Philip asked the question he did?_____

    _____

3. How can you discover what God is like?_____

    _____

COMMENTS

Jesus gives three transitive verbs for which both He and the Father are the proper objects. To *know* Jesus is to know the Father (v. 7); to *see* Jesus is to see the Father (v. 9). To *believe* in the Father, you should also believe in Jesus (v. 1). The reason for this is found in the statement, "I am in the Father, and the Father in me." When Jesus answered Thomas' question about the way, He included the end of the way, God the Father, and He said that He Himself *was* the way.

These words interested the practical-minded Philip. He anticipated a physical view of God, and he asked for what we all might like—faith based on sight. We always suspect that something more might be done to make God known. But if God were to make a further revelation of Himself to man, what would He do? We know what He has done: He has shown Himself in Jesus Christ.

APPLICATION

1. Here are the three titles Jesus takes to Himself; record the difference these titles make to you as a follower of Christ.

   a. The Way:_____

   b. The Truth:_____

   c. The Life:_____

2. What has Jesus revealed to you about the Father recently?

_____

FURTHER STUDY

1. "Why Believe in Jesus Christ?" in *Why Believe?* by A. Rendle Short, pages 28-55.
2. *Basic Christianity,* pages 21-22.

STUDY **A**

THE DEITY OF JESUS CHRIST

DAY **5**

Jesus' relationship to God

John 5:17-40

QUESTIONS

1. What evidence is given that Jesus is God's equal?_____

_____

_____

2. What does Jesus say is the most valid evidence of His close relationship with God?_____

_____

What use does Jesus make of miracles?_____

_____

3. What is Christ's part in the relationship between God and man?_____

_____

COMMENTS

The Jews understood that Jesus was claiming equality with God (v. 18). Therefore, He was faced with the problem of giving evidence for His claim. How could He, a man, convince others that He was also God? He could give no evidence in His own defense. Such evidence would be invalid, since in Jewish custom the evidence of two or three witnesses is required.

Jesus finds verification for His claim from God (v. 32). God's witness is shown in the works which He has given Jesus to do. Here is evidence that is visible to the Jews, if they would accept it. Jesus also finds a human witness, John the Baptist. He does not place too much weight on this witness, but there is the possibility that some who had been influenced by John, even though it was only "for a while," might respond to this reminder.

APPLICATION

1. Christ says He judges fairly. What does this mean in your life

   a. for your comfort?_____

   _____

   b. for your discomfort?_____

   _____

   What does *justice* mean to God?_____

   _____

2. What is the result of a postive response to Jesus' teaching (v. 24)?_____

   _____

   How have you responded to Jesus' words?_____
   What confidence do you have if you believe Jesus?_____

   _____

   _____

3. The Jews studied the Scriptures diligently because they placed their hope for eternal life in them, but they missed that life because they allowed the Scriptures to block them from Jesus. What actions or attitudes toward the Scriptures are inhibiting your full appreciation of Him?_____

   _____

   _____

1. On the value of miracles as evidence of Jesus' deity, *Basic Christianity*, pages 32-33.
2. "The Miracles of Jesus Christ," in *Son of Man* (Wolff), pages 49-60.
3. On the possibility of miracles, *Miracles*, by C. S. Lewis.
4. What do you think of the statement, "Jesus is God"? Is this accurate? What are the limitations of such a statement? Is it supportable from the New Testament?

STUDY **A**

THE DEITY OF JESUS CHRIST

Colossians 1:15-20
Philippians 2:8-11
Hebrews 1:1-13

DAY **6**

Paul's claims
about Jesus

QUESTIONS

1. What teachings concerning Christ's earthly and divine nature while He was on earth are given in these passages?_____

_____

_____

_____

2. What is Christ's relationship to the church, indeed to everything that exists?_____

_____

What is the meaning of the name *Lord?* What does this relationship tell you about His deity?_____

_____

COMMENTS

Our Lord's intrinsic deity is expressed in language which is probably as strong as any that could be used. Paul does not simply say, "He was God"; he says, "He was in the form of God," and thus emphasizes our Lord's possession of the specific quality of God. The word *form* expresses the sum of those characteristic qualities which make a thing the precise thing that it is. For example, the form of a sword—primarily its external configuration—is all that makes a given piece of metal specifically a sword rather than a spade.[3]

The form of God is the sum of characteristics which make the being called *God* specifically God, and not some other being, an angel or a man, for instance. The statement that Jesus Christ is in the "the form of God" is therefore a most explicit declaration that He is all that God is and that He possesses the whole fullness of attributes which make God, God.[4]

APPLICATION

1. Philippians 2 tells of Christ's great unselfishness toward us. In what ways can you emulate this example?_____

_____

_____

2. As you realize that nothing can happen outside the framework of Christ, how does this affect your evaluation of each part of your life?_____

_____

_____

How can this give you confidence in prayer?_____

_____

_____

3. How has your understanding of Christ's deity enlarged this week?_____

_____

_____

[3]B. B. Warfield, *The Person and Work of Christ* (Nutley, New Jersey: Presbyterian and Reformed Publishing Co., 1950).
[4]*Ibid.*

4. How do you acknowledge in your own experience the fact that Jesus has been given that name which is above every name: *Lord*?_____

_____

_____

FURTHER STUDY
1. Christ's becoming man: II Corinthians 8:9.
2. Christ's human nature: Romans 8:3, I Corinthians 15:21.
3. A difference between Christ and other human beings: I Corinthians 15:47, John 3:13, Ephesians 4:9.
4. Christ's deity: Colossians 2:9, I John 5:20.
5. *Christian Beliefs,* by I. Howard Marshall, pages 45-48.
6. "The Lord of Glory" in *The Lord from Heaven* (Morris), especially pages 72-74.

STUDY **B**

THE LORDSHIP
OF JESUS CHRIST

Luke 5:1-11

DAY **1**

*the call
to discipleship*

QUESTIONS

1. Use your imagination to empathize with Peter. How would you feel as Jesus approached?_____

_____

How might you respond to Jesus' request for the boat?_____

_____

_____

What brought forth Peter's words, "Depart from me, for I am a sinful man"?_____

_____

_____

2. Consider what it meant to Peter to be obedient to Jesus' command in an area where Peter was the expert and when it was against his better judgment to follow the command. Why did he obey?_____

_____

_____

3. What does the difference in Peter's names for Christ in verses 5 and 8 indicate?_____

_____

_____

COMMENTS

Our attention is drawn to the fact that Jesus seeks the disciples and does not wait until they approach Him of their own impulse. He takes the first step toward them; afterwards He can say to them, "You did not choose me, but I chose you. . . ." After Peter's response to Jesus, it is Jesus who indicates what it will mean for Peter: ". . . you will be catching men."

There is no bargain to be struck between Jesus and those whom He calls. Jesus assigns the future to His disciples. He is always the active one. Perhaps Peter's immediate willingness to follow Jesus indicates a new confidence in Him: since Jesus was able to direct the fishing venture successfully, He could also be trusted to order other matters correctly.

APPLICATION

1. Give specific examples from the Gospels of Christ's judgment as compared with that of others._____

_____

_____

_____

Can you have the confidence in Christ which would lead you to obey Him in all matters, even against your better judgment? Why?_____

_____

_____

2. Does Jesus cause you to recognize your own sinfulness?
How? Does this happen often?_____

_____

_____

_____

FURTHER STUDY

The main critical question about this passage is whether
this occurrence is identical with the calling of four disciples,
which is related by Matthew (4:18-22) and Mark (1:16-20),
or whether it is distinct from this and occurred later. The dis-
tinction between the narrative of Luke and that of the other
writers is so great that many have maintained the latter opinion.
What do you think about the probability of such a repetition?
Are there any clear contradictions between the divergent accounts? What are we to think of such divergent accounts in the
Gospels? John 1:35-51 also tells about a confrontation between
Jesus and some of these disciples. How does this fit in? Consider Luke 1:1-4 and John 20:30-31.

STUDY **B**
THE LORDSHIP
OF JESUS CHRIST

Luke 18:18-30

DAY **2**

*morality
and discipleship*

QUESTIONS

1. What does the ruler's question (v. 18) reveal about him?

_____

_____

What does his answer to Jesus reveal about him?_____

_____

_____

2. What did the ruler lack?_____

_____

How did Jesus point this out?_____

_____

Why did Jesus make discipleship so difficult for this eager man?

_____

_____

_____

3. What is the relationship between morality (obedience to commandments of God, charity, etc.) and discipleship?_____

_____

_____

_____

5. Write a summary of the implications of obeying the command: *Follow me.*_____

_____

_____

_____

_____

_____

COMMENTS

We should be quick to acknowledge the ruler's sincerity in his approach to Jesus, although he may have had a superficial view of all that the commandments require (see Matthew 5:21-48). Jesus lists the commandments which underscore our duty to other people rather than to God, but He significantly omits the last one, the prohibition of covetousness. It is this last command that condemns the ruler. He loves money and covets wealth. Paul equates this with idolatry in Colossians 3:5.

We cannot consider the command of verse 22 as binding on all Christians, but is not materialism a vulnerable point for many Americans? The important, universal command here is in the words, "follow me." Jesus is not extolling poverty, but simply pointing out that the ruler's desire for money was greater than his desire to follow Christ. The ruler sought a means of security other than Christ, but the only security Christ offers is Himself.

APPLICATION
1. What might be prohibiting you from following Christ?

_____

_____

What would it mean for you to pass the test of self-renunciation?

_____

_____

_____

2. Are you relying on anything other than Jesus for your security (grades, approval of others, prospect of marriage, girl friend or boy friend)?_____

_____

_____

3. What consolation does this passage give to you?_____

_____

_____

FURTHER STUDY

1. Parallel accounts: Matthew 19:16-30, Mark 10:17-31.

2. It has been suggested that the question which Jesus asks in verse 19 casts doubt upon His sinlessness, and probably upon His deity, either directly or indirectly. There is, however, an alternative to this suggestion. Jesus presses the full meaning of the ruler's adjective *good*, when used of Himself. He is testing the confession of the ruler that Jesus is good, and therefore divine. "If I accepted your form of address," Jesus is saying, "I should be declaring my deity. I accept it." Perhaps the ruler had been careless in his use of *good*. Jesus reminds him that God is the only source of good. Even His own goodness is derived from His union with the Father, as He said in John 5:19.

STUDY **B**

THE LORDSHIP
OF JESUS CHRIST

Luke 9:23-27, 57-62

DAY **3**

*demands
of discipleship, I
(attitudes
toward self)*

QUESTIONS

1. What does the word *if* (v. 23) imply?_____

_____

_____

What three things are demanded of Jesus' followers? What is the

meaning of each?_____

_____

_____

_____

2. What, does Jesus indicate, is the advantage of following

Him?_____

_____

Is this an unfortunate use of the benefit (or fear) motive in

Christianity? Why or why not?_____

_____

_____

3. Compare and contrast the three men in verses 57-62 as to:

a. the opening of their conversations_____

_____

_____

b. the men's attitudes_____

_____

_____

c. Jesus' replies_____

_____

_____

Why did Jesus reply as He did to each?_____

_____

_____

_____

COMMENTS

Jesus' statement of the demands of discipleship follows two significant occurrences. Peter has just acknowledged Jesus' identity (v. 20), and Jesus has given a prediction of His death and resurrection (v. 22). He then indicates that the necessity of suffering in obedience to God's will is laid not only on Him, but also on His followers.

Jesus gives the freedom of choice to His disciples. He does not force them to follow Him, but He makes His demands clear. First, there is self-denial. "To deny oneself is to be aware only of Christ and no more of self, to see only Him who goes before and no more the road which is too hard for us."[5]

Second, one must take up his cross daily. Here a death—either physical or otherwise—in indicated. The disciples understood the implications of a cross since the cross was the cus-

[5]Dietrich Bonhoeffer, *The Cost of Discipleship* (New York: Macmillan Co., 1963), p. 97. Used by permission.

tomary means of capital punishment in their area. They knew that a man who was carrying his cross to his execution could not go where he wanted to go, but moved at someone else's wishes; he could not call anything his own; he could not have any plans for his future.

Third, there is the call to follow Christ. Some of the implications of following Christ are indicated in the second passage (vv. 57-62). Jesus cautions against over-zealousness that does not weigh the difficulties. He demands immediate action, overruling the restrictions of societal mores. He rejects any bargaining attempt, expecting His followers to come on His terms.

APPLICATION

1. How can you respond to Jesus' call?_____

_____

What is the meaning of *cross* for you? Be specific._____

_____

_____

2. What would the conversation be like if you were in the place of one of the men in verses 57-62? What would Jesus have to say to you?_____

_____

_____

_____

FURTHER STUDY

1. *Cost of Discipleship,* by Dietrich Bonhoeffer, pages 64-67, 95-101.
2. *Sacrifice,* by Howard W. Guinness.

STUDY **B**
THE LORDSHIP
OF JESUS CHRIST

Luke 14:25-35

DAY **4**

demands
of discipleship, II
(attitudes toward
possessions)

QUESTIONS

1. What were the circumstances of Jesus' addressing the crowd?

_____

_____

_____

2. In what context does Jesus use the word *hate*, and why is it necessary that He use this term? What does *hate* mean in this context?_____

_____

_____

3. In what ways are the parables of the tower builder and the king analogous to the Christian life?_____

_____

_____

_____

4. What does it mean to "renounce all" (v. 33, RSV)?_____

_____

_____

COMMENTS

Jesus' call is to the individual, and He expects individual response. Every man is called separately and must follow alone. Jesus brings each person into direct contact with Himself, compelling the individual to accept and affirm his own break with the world and with his past. This passage is "perhaps the supreme instance of His statement of the terms of discipleship. In the course of His words there is a thrice-repeated phrase, 'cannot be My disciple,' . . . and in connection with it a revelation of the only terms upon which men may be His disciples."[6] The word *hate* is used as the opposite of love. Christ is stressing a principle which must control the disciple's loyalty.

We cannot justify *direct* relationship with the things of the world, as if they deserved our direct allegiance or were our own rights, if we are to be disciples. When we offer thanks for the gifts that God has given us we do so *through* Jesus Christ. "And whatever you do, in word or deed, do everything in the name of the Lord Jesus, giving thanks to God the Father through him" (Colossians 3:17). A balance must be struck between extreme self-denial (asceticism) and self-gratification.

APPLICATION

1. With what things are you having a direct relationship rather than obtaining them in and through Jesus Christ?_____

_____

What are you not prepared to "hate" in the way that Jesus requires (car, stereo, grades)?_____

_____

2. What are the "ears" of verse 35, and who has them?_____

_____

[6]G. Campbell Morgan, *The Gospel According to Luke* (Westwood, New Jersey: Fleming H. Revell Company), p. 175. Used by permission.

Is it possible that you are hearing without responding to Jesus?

_____

_____

3. How would an awareness of the obligations of discipleship affect your life?_____

_____

_____

FURTHER STUDY
1. *Cost of Discipleship* (Bonhoeffer), chapter five.
2. "Counting the Cost," in *Basic Christianity,* pages 109-121.
3. *The Gospel According to Luke,* by G. Campbell Morgan, pages 174-179.

STUDY **B**
THE LORDSHIP
OF JESUS CHRIST

John 14:12-24

DAY **5**

*the disciple's
relation to Christ*

QUESTIONS

1. What promises and privilege does Jesus make available to His disciples in verses 12-14? _____

_____

_____

2. How does the privilege of prayer make it possible for the disciple to do "greater things" than Jesus did? _____

_____

_____

3. What particular thing mentioned in this passage is necessary in order for a relationship to be established between the Father and the disciple? _____

What is this love? _____

_____

4. What are the characteristics of the relationship between Jesus and the Father, and you (v. 23)? _____

_____

How is this verse an especially good expression of what it means to be a Christian?_____

_____

_____

COMMENTS

It would be easy to become legalistic about the relationship of a disciple to his lord, or to view discipleship as merely hard and demanding. This passage gives the balance so that discipleship is viewed properly. Here Jesus expresses the warmth of His love and His relationship with His disciples. He indicates that His disciples are acting in His place on the earth, doing His works and even greater things. They act and pray in His name; that is, they do what He would do and pray what He would pray.

Jesus' life and prayers were characterized by His obedience to God. ". . . I always do what pleases him," He said (John 8:29, Phillips). The disciple who is acting in Jesus' name must therefore be guided by complete obedience to God's will. Such obedience will grow not from mere legalism and volition, but from the warm love of the disciple for his Lord. Love that issues in obedience (v. 23) brings the most intimate relationship between God and man.

APPLICATION

1. If Jesus has come into your life, how has it been affected?

_____

_____

_____

2. Are you aware of acting in Jesus' name in all that you do?

_____

How does such awareness differentiate your action from that of others?_____

_____

_____

3. What functions does Jesus say the Holy Spirit performs?

_____

_____

_____

What difference is the Holy Spirit making in your life?_____

_____

_____

_____

FURTHER STUDY

1. How would you use the material from this study to answer these questions:
    a. What is a Christian?
    b. How can I become a Christian?

John 21:15-22

QUESTIONS

1. What does Jesus equate with love for Him? _____

_____

2. Why do you think Christ repeated His question to Peter three times? (Compare John 13:38.) _____

_____

_____

3. Why does Jesus say, "Follow me," immediately after He has indicated that Peter will be martyred? _____

_____

_____

COMMENTS

Almost three years stand between this incident and the one we studied on the first day of this week. Peter spent most of that time in the close company of Jesus. Just days before this incident, however, Peter denied any relationship with Jesus. Now Jesus comes to a humiliated Peter and asks if there is still some love in Peter for Him. Peter indicates that there is. If there is this love,

Jesus says, it will manifest itself in service to others. Without this love, obedience to Jesus will be impossible.

The going will not become easier for Peter; in fact, it will become harder, and Peter will finally be killed for his Christian profession—perhaps the very thing Peter had feared when he denied Jesus. But Jesus renews His invitation to Peter: "Follow me." What an encouragement to know that if even one kernel of love remains in us after we fail to live up to Christ's demands for our discipleship, Jesus stands ready to renew His invitation to us.

APPLICATION

1. Is it ever necessary for Jesus to be repetitious with you as He was with Peter? Why?_____

_____

_____

2. Are you now in need of returning to the Lord Jesus? Can you find the encouragement here to return immediately? Explain.

_____

_____

_____

3. What do you learn from verses 18-23 about the individuality of the Lord's call to His disciples?_____

_____

_____

What legitimate concern do you have for the way in which the Lord is directing someone else?_____

_____

_____

What do you learn about being sure that you are following the Lord yourself, no matter how others may be led?_____

_____

_____

_____

4. What have you learned this week about the meaning of the word *Lord* and of the statement, "Jesus Christ is Lord" (Philippians 2:11)?_____

_____

_____

_____

FURTHER STUDY

1. In what sense is it true that Christianity is the only religion derived from the *identity* of its founder?
2. *Christianity is Christ,* by W. H. Griffeth Thomas.

STUDY **C**
THE LOVE OF
JESUS CHRIST

Luke 7:36-50

DAY **1**

Jesus and sinners

1. Contrast the responses of Jesus and Simon to the woman in this passage. _____

_____

_____

Why did Jesus act the way He did toward her?_____

_____

_____

2. Contrast the responses of the woman and of Simon to Jesus.

_____

_____

_____

In what sense did Simon see little need of forgiveness?_____

_____

_____

3. What is the relationship between love and forgiveness?_____

_____

4. Did the people in Simon's house understand what Jesus was saying? Explain._____

_____

What do you think they might have been discussing as they left Simon's house?_____

_____

COMMENTS

In this passage, Jesus clearly indicates His love for both Simon and the woman. He does not differentiate between the sin of Simon's smugness and the woman's immorality. He knows that these are outward manifestations of sin within the heart. Notice how kindly Christ seeks to help Simon understand this concept. Jesus desires that Simon realize that his legal righteousness will not get recognition from God. He wanted Simon to *see* as God sees. Simon thinks Jesus cannot see what the woman is, but Jesus tells Simon of his own blindness to what the woman has become since her sins are forgiven. She *was* what Simon sees; she *is* what Jesus sees.

The woman recognized her sins and responded to Jesus. Christ's forgiveness inspired her to show through action her love for Him. Simon was not aware of his need of forgiveness; therefore, he did not manifest love. Simon was the victim of the legalism of his peers and thought he could obtain God's favor by his legal righteousness. It is only when we recognize that God loves us freely and forgives us in Christ, regardless of our deeds, that torrents of love can flow from us to Him.

APPLICATION
1. What is your view of God?_____

_____

_____

What does your attitude toward God do within you?_____

_____

2. In what ways does His forgiveness inspire love in you?_____

_____

_____

3. In your relationships with others, how can you imitate Jesus' attitude toward the woman?_____

_____

_____

How can you imitate Jesus' attitude toward Simon?_____

_____

_____

4. What is the basis for accepting non-Christians?_____

_____

_____

FURTHER STUDY
1. On forgiveness: Matthew 6:14, Luke 6:37, Luke 11:4.
2. On relationship to sinners: Matthew 9:10-13, 11:19.
3. Our conduct is largely determined by our view of the nature of God. How is this true religiously? ethically?

STUDY **C**

**THE LOVE OF
JESUS CHRIST**

Luke 15:1-32

DAY **2**

Jesus and the lost

QUESTIONS

1. What occurrences precipitated Jesus' telling of these three parables? _____

_____

_____

2. There are certain parallels among the parables (vv. 3-7, 8-10, 11-24). To see these, fill out the following chart.

	VERSES 3-7	VERSES 8-10	VERSES 11-24
SITUATION:	_____	_____	_____
	_____	_____	_____
SUBJECTS: (PERSONS AND THINGS)	_____	_____	_____
	_____	_____	_____
EVENTS:	_____	_____	_____
	_____	_____	_____
RESULTS:	_____	_____	_____
	_____	_____	_____

PRINCIPAL
IDEAS: _____   _____   _____

            _____   _____   _____

            _____   _____   _____

3. What do these parables mean? (In interpreting a parable, generally look for only one main idea. Use your answer to question one to help you discover the meaning of the parables.)

_____

_____

_____/_____

What is taught here about the nature of true love?_____

_____

_____

4. Imaginatively project yourself into the person of the older brother. How did he respond? Why?_____

_____

_____

How is the older brother like Simon in yesterday's selection? How is he like the Pharisees of verse 2?_____

_____

_____

COMMENTS

These parables are not primarily about lost items, but about people (a shepherd, a woman, and a father) who are seeking lost items. Helmut Thielicke has entitled the third parable, not "The Prodigal Son," but "The Waiting Father." Jesus was criticized by the religious leaders for His associations with undesirables, but Jesus demonstrated that in these associations with sinners He was seeking those who needed Him most.

The Jewish leaders were rightly concerned for their moral purity, but in their zeal, they had forgotten the need for love. Jesus shows His love for sinners by going to where they are and identifying with them so that they will learn from experience what God's love and forgiveness are. The Jewish leaders thought they should separate themselves physically from sinners. Jesus showed that true love goes out to the sinner because of its concern for him, and that physical association with sinners need not indicate approval for their actions.

APPLICATION

1. What do you learn about Jesus from this chapter?_____

_____

About God? _____

_____

2. Do you act as Jesus did in this chapter? Do you associate much with those who need you and your Savior?_____

_____

Why might you not do this?_____

_____

What should you do?_____

_____

FURTHER STUDY

1. In a Bible dictionary, look up *scribe, Pharisees, Sadducees, publicans,* and *sinners.* This background will enrich your understanding of these parables. (*The New Bible Dictionary* is recommended.)
2. Study the laws of Jewish inheritance. Look up *heir* and *inheritance.*

STUDY **C**
**THE LOVE OF
JESUS CHRIST**

John 15:1-17

DAY **3**
fellowship with Jesus

QUESTIONS
1. What does Jesus teach here about the demands of discipleship and the conditions under which it is effective?

_____

_____

_____

2. What results can be expected if one abides in Christ?_____

_____

_____

3. Define *abide* in this context. What does it involve?

_____

_____

_____

4. What part does Jesus' teaching play in the relationship described by this metaphor?_____

_____

_____

COMMENTS

Love and obedience are complementary. Jesus obeyed His Father because there is a mutual and permanent love between Him and the Father. In the same way, obedience is not possible to His disciples unless they love Jesus and are aware of His love for them, nor is it consistent for His disciples to affirm love for Jesus without obeying Him. Jesus wants us to enjoy continually His love for us; thus He warns us to be careful not to deprive ourselves of it.

The obedience which the disciple gives is not so much the cause of Jesus' love as it is the effect. But it may seem that the condition of obedience imposed on us is too difficult. We know ourselves to be far short of the perfection that Christ commands us to have (Matthew 5:48), but we need not be discouraged unless we view this too legalistically, for example, by believing our obedience merits His love. Disciples are "regarded as keeping Christ's commandments when they apply themselves to them, though they be far distant from their mark."[7]

APPLICATION

1. Are you aware of abiding in Christ? Explain. _____

_____

_____

2. How does the love of Christ assist you in obeying Him?

_____

_____

_____

3. What relationship do you see between forgiveness, love, and

[7]John Calvin, *New Testament Commentaries, The Gospel According to St. John,* Vol. 2 (Grand Rapids: Eerdmans Publishing Co., 1961), p. 98. Used by permission.

obedience? In what ways do you see this relationship in your life?

_____

_____

_____

_____

FURTHER STUDY

The metaphor of the vine to describe the people God loves is not original in John 15. It was used in the Old Testament to describe the people of God. This may help you to understand why Jesus chose the vine to portray His people. Jeremiah called the nation of Israel, God's chosen people, "a choice vine, of pure seed, which became degenerate, a wild vine" (Jeremiah 2:21). Psalm 80 describes this vine as having been brought from Egypt (v. 8) and especially cultivated (v. 9). The fifth chapter of Isaiah describes God's relationship with His people as that of a gardener to a vineyard. Why is this metaphor so fitting for depicting the relationship between God and His people?

STUDY **C**
THE LOVE OF
JESUS CHRIST

John 15:12-27

DAY **4**

*the love of Jesus and
our love for others*

QUESTIONS

1. Jesus suggests that the disciples' relationship to Him may be that of servants or friends. Contrast the roles of servants and friends._____

_____

_____

_____

2. What is the chief characteristic of a friendship, and how is it most strikingly shown?_____

_____

Why are the opening and closing sentences of the first paragraph (vv. 12 and 17) the same?_____

_____

_____

3. What is the relationship of the world, Jesus, and the disciples?_____

_____

Why is it this way?_____

_____

COMMENTS

Jesus has just declared that obedience to His commands is a prerequisite and a result of abiding in His love. But, we might ask, which of His commands shall we obey most carefully? Jesus singles out His most crucial command: "Love one another." Only minutes before, Jesus called this a "new commandment" (John 13:34-35). Love, He said, would distinguish them as His disciples to everyone. This love is no mere acceptance or enjoyment of another, but makes sacrifices for the benefit of the loved person, even to the point of death.

A striking description of love is given by Paul in I Corinthians 13—love which "seeks not her own." It does not even claim what is rightfully its own, but gives up its rights. Jesus' complete sacrifice of Himself for us dramatizes this love. Jesus does not require of us what He has not already done for us. Thus Paul can say, " . . . try to be like him, and live in love as Christ loved you, and gave himself up on your behalf as an offering . . . (Ephesians 5:1-2 NEB).

APPLICATION

1. In what ways does Jesus' demonstration of love help you to love?_____

_____

_____

2. At what point does your concern (love) for other Christians stop, and refuse to give any more?_____

_____

_____

What rights do you feel you should protect from the interference of others?_____

_____

_____

3. How would your opinion that another Christian has betrayed your sacrificial love or that he is not worthy of your love modify your exercise of love toward him? (Think of how the disciples—and even we—betrayed Jesus' love.)_____

_____

_____

_____

FURTHER STUDY

Compare verse 22 with John 9:39-41. What does this teach about the relationship between opportunity and liability? Christ is thinking here of the Jewish people to whom God had especially revealed Himself and His truth. But their rejection of Jesus was a rejection of the God they claimed to serve. This action might be expected from pagans, but it was inexcusable among Jews. They maliciously and willfully refused to recognize Jesus' divine origin and nature.

STUDY **C**
THE LOVE OF
JESUS CHRIST

John 16:16-28

DAY **5**

*Jesus
and his disciples*

We are again looking in on Jesus' last night with His disciples prior to His crucifixion. His relationship with, and love for, His disciples is evident to us as we study what He says and does.

1. How does Jesus prepare the disciples for His death? Note verses 16, 20, and 22. _____

_____

_____

_____

2. After the sorrowful period is over, the disciples will have new blessings and privileges. Jesus mentions at least four in these verses. What are they?_____

_____

_____

_____

3. What has brought about a relationship of love between the Father and the disciples?_____

_____

What should be the result of this relationship? _____

_____

COMMENTS

"In my name"—this phrase occurs in three verses of this section. It illustrates one of the most staggering truths that confront us in Scripture, and represents a tremendous privilege as well as a responsibility. Think, for a moment, of an ambassador of the government of the United States to another country. In the exercise of his duties he does not act in his own name; when he speaks, he is speaking in the name of the American people. He says what he thinks his government and his countrymen would say if they were in his place. His words have authority equal, not to his intrinsic authority, but to the merits of the name in which he is acting, namely, the United States of America.

Now transfer these thoughts to the realm of acting and praying in Jesus' name. We approach the Father and are received by Him not because of any intrinsic worth in us, but because of the merits of the One who is our Friend, the Father's Son. Accordingly, when we speak to God, we must say those things which we think Jesus would say if He were speaking. (Compare Study B, Day 5.)

APPLICATION

1. How does the thought of praying in Jesus' name affect the way you pray? _____

_____

2. Do you know how to pray and what to pray for, in Jesus' name? How can you learn this? _____

_____

_____

3. What do you mean when you end your prayers, "In Jesus'

name?" _____

_____

_____

FURTHER STUDY

1. The death of Christ, and His "departure to the Father, so far from ending His influence on earth, will mean its continuance under wider conditions and with results rendered possible by the power of effective prayer."[8] Note how this is true in John 14:12-13. Luke implies, in Acts 1:1, that the work done by the apostles was, in fact, what Jesus was continuing to do (note *began*) because the apostles were acting in His name.

2. *Prayer,* by O. Hallesby.

3. "Prayer" in *IVCF Guide to Campus Christian Life,* pages 15-17.

[8]R. G. V. Tasker, *Commentary on the Gospel According to St. John* (Grand Rapids: Eerdmans Publishing Co., 1960), p. 166. Used by permission.

STUDY **C**

THE LOVE OF
JESUS CHRIST

John 13:1-20

DAY **6**

love demonstrated

QUESTIONS

1. What do the verbs *knew* and *loved* in verse one reveal about Jesus?_____

_____

How does He refer to the disciples?_____

_____

2. Why does it seem that Jesus was performing an incongruous act in washing the disciples' feet?_____

_____

_____

3. Why did Peter not want Jesus to wash his feet?_____

_____

4. What lesson does Jesus draw from His act of washing the disciples' feet. _____

_____

Is Christ's sovereignty lessened by this act? Consider I Peter 5:4-5, and explain._____

56

_____

_____

_____

5. Why did Jesus say to Peter, ". . . you are clean, but not all of you"? What does this teach us about spiritual cleansing?

_____

_____

_____

_____

COMMENTS

Jesus' lessons for His disciples were not always easy; sometimes, as on this occasion, they were very painful. On the night before His death Jesus demonstrates His care and thoughtfulness toward the disciples in a striking way. Every act of that last evening demonstrated His lack of self-pity through conscious and ultimate acts of love for others. Knox translates part of the first verse, "he gave them the uttermost proof of his love"—the performance of a most menial act of service.

This act was particularly striking because, as Luke tells us (Luke 22:24-27), some of the disciples had been disputing about which of them was to be regarded as the greatest. Jesus put an end to their dispute: "let the greatest among you become as the youngest, and the leader as one who serves . . . But I am among you as one who serves." By serving He was an example of His teaching.

From this dramatic lesson, Jesus intended His disciples to learn the blessings of service, not only as an inspiring thought, but as a practice (v. 17). It is not enough to recognize our obligation to serve. We must respond with positive action. Tasker says, "The primary basis of Christian ethics is the example of Christ Himself. 'If I then, your Lord and Master, have washed your feet; ye also ought to wash one another's feet.' The servant who has been rendered such a supreme act of service by Him whom he rightly calls 'Lord and Master' cannot be exempt from the duty of loving his fellow-servants; to claim such exemption would be to assert that he was greater than his Lord."[9]

APPLICATION

1. In what ways can you follow Jesus' example as given in this passage?_____

_____

_____

Where have you recently failed to serve?_____

_____

_____

2. What is your attitude toward serving others?_____

_____

How do you serve others?_____

_____

3. What have you learned about the love of Jesus this week?

_____

_____

[9]*Ibid.*, p. 156. Used by permission.

STUDY **D**

THE DEATH
OF JESUS CHRIST

DAY **1**

*Jesus meets
man's needs*

QUESTIONS

The studies for this week center around what Jesus Christ, through His death, has done for men. Historically, the Christian Church has held that the most significant moment of Jesus' life on earth was the moment of His death. We shall study Jesus' view of the significance of His death tomorrow. In both His life and death, Jesus was acting to meet the needs of men. He can still meet men's needs because He is alive today. In today's study we shall note some of man's needs which Jesus meets.

1. Turn to the indicated passages. Find what is implied or stated in each as to the need of man, and the way that Jesus meets that need.

PASSAGE	MAN'S NEEDS	JESUS' SOLUTION
a. John 10:11-15	_____	_____
	_____	_____
	_____	_____
b. Luke 19:10	_____	_____
	_____	_____
	_____	_____

c. Matthew 9:12 _____ _____

_____ _____

_____ _____

d. John 8:12 _____ _____

_____ _____

_____ _____

e. Matthew 1:21 _____ _____
   (John 1:29) _____ _____

f. John 6:35 _____ _____
   (John 4:13-14) _____ _____
   (John 7:38-39) _____ _____

_____ _____

g. John 11:25-26 _____ _____

_____ _____

_____ _____

h. Matthew 11:28-30 _____ _____

_____ _____

_____ _____

i. John 14:6 _____ _____

_____ _____

_____ _____

j. John 8:31-36 _____ _____

_____ _____

_____ _____

2. In your school today the students manifest some basic needs. Some of these needs are listed below. Beside each need, place

the number or numbers of passages above which indicate Jesus' ability to meet the respective needs.

Lack of peace	_____	Need to succeed	_____
Guilt	_____	Lack of self-control leading to inability to be moral	_____
Purposelessness (feeling lost)	_____		
Emptiness (desire for reality)	_____	Uncertainty (for example, about world conditions)	_____
Desire for truth	_____	Identity crisis (Who am I?)	_____
Lack of dates	_____		
Loneliness	_____	Desire for immortality	_____

APPLICATION

1. What are the needs in your life which Jesus can meet, but is not yet meeting? _____

_____

_____

Why is this? _____

_____

_____

2. What needs has Jesus met for you already? Thank Him for these. _____

_____

_____

3. What individual can you direct to Jesus so that He can meet his needs? _____

_____

_____

STUDY **D**
THE DEATH
OF JESUS CHRIST

DAY **2**

*Jesus' view
of his death*

Mark 10:35-45

QUESTIONS

1. Describe the situation and attitudes that brought on Jesus' teaching in verses 43-45. _____

_____

_____

_____

2. What two purposes does Jesus give for His life?_____

_____

Are these really two, or essentially one?_____

_____

3. What do verses 39 and 45 show about Jesus' consciousness of His coming death?_____

_____

_____

4. Turn to Matthew 16:21-23. What does this section show about Jesus' consciousness of His death? What does the *must*

of verse 21 imply? (See also Matthew 17:22-23 and 20:17-19.)

_____

_____

_____

_____

5. Read Matthew 26:28. What does Jesus see as the significance of His death? Comment on the word *many* in comparison with Mark 10:45._____

_____

_____

_____

COMMENTS

"When Jesus came, He knew Himself to be a son of destiny."[10] In His mind, His death was the focal point of His life. All other men live for what can be accomplished in their lives; Jesus lived for what could be accomplished in His death. It was His death that Jesus called "my hour." Jesus was conscious that His death was to be at an appointed time when He said, "My hour is not yet come" (John 7:6-8). Although there were attempts to kill Jesus prior to that, these attempts were frustrated "because his hour had not yet come" (John 7:30, 8:20). The ultimate disclosure of the meaning of Jesus' hour came the night prior to His death. Then He said, "The hour has come" (John 17:1). Earlier the same evening, with His death in view, He had prayed, "Now is my soul troubled; and what shall I say? Father, save me from this hour: but for this cause came I unto this hour" (John 12:27).

[10]J. R. W. Stott, *Basic Christianity* (Chicago: Inter-Varsity Press, 1958), p. 83.

FURTHER STUDY

1. *The Death of Christ,* by James Denney, pages 17-40, is a complete and precise study of Jesus' view of His death.

2. Jesus' view of His death is by no means an unimportant study. Modern scholarship has been prone to say that traditional beliefs concerning the meaning of Jesus' death are products of the minds of theologians rather than consistent with Jesus' own view of His death. Can we say that Jesus was unaware that His death was for the redemption of mankind? Would Jesus have agreed with Paul when he said, "But God commendeth His love toward us, in that, while we were yet sinners, Christ died for us" (Romans 5:8)?

STUDY **D**

THE DEATH
OF JESUS CHRIST

DAY **3**

Jesus' last words

QUESTIONS

Our study today is based on the seven remarks of Jesus Christ on the cross. He spoke His last recorded sentences between approximately 9 A.M. and His death at 3 P.M. (9 A.M. to 12 noon—remarks a-c; 12-3 P.M.—three hours of darkness; approximately 3 P.M.—remarks d-g). The order in which these words were spoken is not completely agreed upon, but the listing here is a good possibility.

1. Read quickly through the following sections: Matthew 27: 27-56, Luke 23:32-49, and John 19:17-30. While you are reading, imagine you are a bystander. What sounds do you hear (for example, the tone of voice with which the words were spoken and the pounding of nails)?_____

_____

_____

2. Complete the following chart:

REMARK OF JESUS CHRIST	WHAT IT REVEALS ABOUT JESUS
a. "Father, forgive them; they do not know what they are doing."	_____ _____

What was happening when He said this?

_____

b. "... today you shall be with me in Paradise."

_____

_____

_____

_____

c. "Mother, there is your son . . . . There is your mother."

_____

_____

_____

_____

d. "My God, my God, why hast Thou forsaken me?"
Was this a carefully studied question, or a cry of anguish from deep suffering?
Did He know the answer?
Why did God forsake Him?

_____

_____

_____

_____

e. "I thirst."

_____

_____

_____

f. "It is accomplished!"

_____

_____

g. "Father, into thy hands I commit my spirit!"

_____

_____

_____

_____

COMMENTS

"Since God cannot look upon sin (Habakkuk 1:13), He hid His face when our sin was laid upon His sinless Son: Jesus, the sinner's substitute and sin-bearer, was in fact forsaken that we might never be (Hebrews 13:5). This was indeed the supreme and unparalleled sorrow from which He shrank."[11]

APPLICATION

1. What is your response to the scene studied today?_____

_____

_____

_____

2. Have you gained a new appreciation of Jesus' death from the study of these words? Explain._____

_____

_____

_____

[11]*The New Bible Commentary*, p. 838. Used by permission.

STUDY **D**

THE DEATH
OF JESUS CHRIST

DAY **4**

Jesus' suffering

Hebrews 2:9-18

QUESTIONS

1. Why did God's Son become man and then die? List the reasons given in this passage._____

_____

_____

What results came from Jesus' death for Himself?_____

_____

_____

_____

What results come for man?_____

_____

_____

_____

2. Compare verse 9 with Philippians 2:8-11. How are the incarnation, the death, and the exaltation of Jesus related?

_____

_____

_____

_____

_____

_____

COMMENTS

The death of Jesus, God's Son, might be viewed as a dishonorable event for God. Indeed, many persons hold this view. The writer of this passage apparently desires to ward off such a contention. In verse 10 he indicates explicitly that it was "fitting" (RSV) or "right and proper" (Phillips) for Christ to endure the humiliation of suffering and death.

Second, he reminds us that the best justification for Christ's humiliation is that this course pleased God. The writer could have used the word *God* in verse 10, but he intended to remind us that whatever God does must be considered best because of who God is and therefore uses "for whom and by whom all things exist." He is the God who does all things according to His own purpose (Ephesians 1:11), and does not do what is unworthy of Himself.

Third, the suffering of Christ gives Him full identification and empathy with those whom He is redeeming (see also Hebrews 5:2-9). "Perfect through suffering" does not indicate that Jesus had moral faults which were corrected. The same writer asserts that Jesus suffered all temptations but was Himself without sin (Hebrews 4:15). The Greek word here translated *perfect* means "to make adequate," or "completely effective." By His full identification with man—in temptations, in suffering, in death—Christ can more effectively represent and help man.

APPLICATION

1. What does it mean to you that Jesus experienced temptation and suffering as you do?_____

_____

_____

2. Think of some specific temptations and difficulties that concern you. Picture Jesus, as a man, also having similar difficulties (similar in nature if not corresponding precisely in detail). In what ways does this give you encouragement?_____

_____

_____

_____

FURTHER STUDY
1. Compare verses 14 and 15 with I Corinthians 15:54-57.
2. "A Great High Priest" in *The Lord from Heaven* (Morris), pages 83-92.

STUDY **D**

THE DEATH
OF JESUS CHRIST

Isaiah 52:13—53:12

DAY **5**

*the meaning
of Jesus' death*

QUESTIONS

The New Testament interprets these verses as a prefiguration of Jesus' death. While Jewish opinions have been diverse, some rabbinical scholars, both before and after the time of Christ, have understood them to refer to the Messiah to come. The fulfillment of the Servant figure in the life and death of Jesus is assumed in our discussion. (See notes in *Further Study*.)

1. List the characteristics of the Servant._____

_____

_____

_____

What is your picture of Him?_____

_____

_____

2. Note the different responses of people to the Servant:

    a. How are the authorities of the world affected? (In verse 15 the RSV word *startle* is a better translation than *sprinkle* in the KJV.) _____

_____

b. What causes men to reject and not believe the story (vv. 1-3)?_____

_____

c. What mistaken notion do some men have (v. 4)?_____

_____

3. Why did the Servant suffer (vv. 5, 6, 10)?_____

_____

_____

4. How do others benefit because the Servant suffers (v. 11)?

_____

_____

5. What is the relationship between the Lord and the Servant in the circumstances described here?_____

_____

_____

6. How does the Servant benefit because He suffers. Compare this with Philippians 2:8-11._____

_____

_____

COMMENTS

This section of the Old Testament is a most crucial one for understanding the New Testament teaching concerning Jesus' death. If we think of the New Testament as the fulfillment of the Old, as Christians always have, Isaiah 53 stands as a bridge between the two. Wright observed that this chapter was "an enigma which could not be fully understood in the days before Christ, but which has been solved by the sufferings, death, resurrection, and exaltation of Him who was both Son of Man and Son of God."[12]

The central truth taught in this passage is that Jesus' death was a substitution. Jesus died when others should have. He was the Innocent One; all others were guilty (v. 6). But the Lord put the guilt of all others to the account of the Innocent One. The fact of Jesus' substitution is indicated in two other figures in this passage: it was a voluntary act in which He made Himself "an offering for sin," and it was a death in which He "bore the sin of many."

APPLICATION

1. What does this study reveal about the character and work of Jesus Christ?_____

_____

_____

_____

2. What is your response to God and Christ after this study?

_____

_____

_____

FURTHER STUDY

1. Does Isaiah 53 apply to Jesus in New Testament thought? Compare Luke 22:37, Acts 8:32-35, and tomorrow's study. See also Matthew 12:17-21 and *Christian Beliefs* (Marshall), page 5. Perhaps Jesus was alluding to the "many" of verses 11 and 12 in Mark 10:45.

2. In today's section there are many allusions to the Jewish

[12]C. H. H. Wright, *The Servant of Jehovah,* quoted in David Baron, *The Servant of Jehovah* (London: Marshall, Morgan and Scott, 1954), p. 10.

religious sacrifices which are not fully comprehensible without an understanding of the Hebrew religion. Study Leviticus 16 and 17. See pages 90-93 of *Basic Christianity* for an explanation of the allusions.

3. This passage was written about 700 years before Jesus' birth. What parallels can you find between this section and the life of Jesus? Compare the following: verse 7 with John 1:29 and 36, verse 12 with Mark 10:45 and Hebrews 9:28, verse 4 with Matthew 8:17, verse 7 with Matthew 26:62-63 and Mark 14:61, verse 9 with Matthew 27:57-60, and verse 9 and 12 with Matthew 27:38. See also Luke 24:44-47.

STUDY **D**

THE DEATH
OF JESUS CHRIST

I Peter 2:21-25
II Corinthians 5:16-21

DAY **6**

*two views
of Jesus' death*

QUESTIONS

1. List the parallel ideas and words about Jesus' death in Peter's writing and the Isaiah passage in yesterday's study._____

_____

_____

_____

_____

2. What reasons and results does Peter give for Christ's death?

_____

_____

_____

_____

3. What is taught about Jesus in each of today's passages?

_____

_____

_____

4. What interpretations of the death of Christ are given in

these sections?_____

_____

_____

COMMENTS

In context, Peter's discussion of the death of Christ follows the fact that Christians are often called to suffer what appear to be unjust difficulties. Here he is speaking to servants who have overbearing masters. In I Peter 3:17 and 18, the death of Jesus is held up as an example for any Christian who suffers for his faith in Christ. Peter gives two principal reasons for the death of Christ: it leaves us an example (v. 21), and Jesus "bore our sins" (v. 24).

The meaning of "to bear sin" may be a bit elusive; it is a Hebraism which Peter used because he was a Jew, and is also used in Hebrews 9:28. The idea contained in this phrase can be discovered by noting several Old Testament references—Leviticus 5:17, Numbers 14:34, and Exodus 28:43—from which we infer that "to bear sin" means to take the consequences of sin, or to be liable for and to suffer the judgment incurred by violation of God's commands. Peter is saying that in His death Christ took upon Himself the consequences of our sins. "To be made sin," as Paul uses the phrase, contains the same idea.

Both Peter and Paul are careful to point out that the One who bore our sins was not Himself liable for punishment for His own sins, since Jesus was innocent and sinless. His sinlessness was symbolized in the Old Testament sacrificial system by the spotless lamb. See Numbers 28:3 and 29:17 and 29; compare these with I Peter 1:18-19.

APPLICATION

1. What examples does Peter indicate that Jesus has set for you? List some modern day situations in which Jesus' examples

can be followed._____

_____

_____

_____

2. On the basis of Jesus' death, what practical result does Peter expect from Christians?_____

_____

What does this mean to you in your daily living?_____

_____

3. What does Paul say in Corinthians about the possibility of living this way?_____

_____

FURTHER STUDY

1. An especially good and concise discussion of this subject may be found in *Basic Christianity,* pages 86-97. Stott says "there is no redemption in an example" (p. 89). Why not? Is it fair for someone else to bear the consequences of our sins?
2. Stott also says, "This simple and wonderful talk of the sin-bearing of the Son of God is strangely unpopular today" (p. 93). Why is this?

STUDY **E**
THE RESURRECTION
OF JESUS CHRIST

DAY **1**

*the resurrection
event, I*

Luke 23:55-24:11

QUESTIONS

"The claims of Jesus to represent the character of God, his claims to be the master of men and of their ultimate destiny, and his claim to be sent by God to effect the reconciliation between man and God would remain as the lunatic arrogance of a disordered mind if everything ended in the judicial murder of a field-preacher on a Roman cross."[13]

1. Why did the women go to the tomb, and what did they expect? _____

_____

_____

_____

2. What evidence in this passage refutes, or tends to refute, the following contentions designed to explain away the resurrection?

    a. The women went to the   _____
    wrong tomb.

                               _____

                               _____

                               _____

[13]J. B. Phillips, *God Our Contemporary* (New York: Macmillan, 1960), pp. 85-86. Used by permission.

b. The disciples wished for the resurrection so much that they deceived themselves, thinking Jesus was alive (that is, they had the "will to believe").

_____

_____

_____

_____

_____

c. They expected Jesus to come back to life and the power of suggestion worked to make them think He had.

_____

_____

_____

_____

3. To what fact did the two men "in dazzling apparel" call the women's attention? What is the significance of this?_____

_____

_____

_____

4. Of what significance is the fact that the women and the disciples did not understand or remember Christ's prediction of His resurrection?_____

_____

_____

COMMENTS

That Jesus predicted His resurrection before His death is a necessary and expected detail. It is clear that neither the women nor the disciples understood nor remembered Christ's prediction. The historical evidence for the prediction, however, compels us to conclude that it was made.

But, it might be asked, could not the early Christians have inserted the predictions into the accounts at a later time for their own advantage? Such a suggestion is put aside by a very unusual bit of evidence: those who accused and tried Jesus unwittingly attested the fact of His prediction. During His trial, while an indictment was being sought for Jesus, "two men alleged that he had said, 'I can pull down the temple of God, and rebuild it in three days' " (Matthew 26:61). Although this accusation was thrown out of court, it has interest for us because it contains the words "in three days." There is significance in this phrase because it occurs elsewhere in Jesus' teaching when He is predicting His resurrection (Mark 8:31, 9:31, 10:33-34). Morison, in his book, *Who Moved the Stone?* says, "When we come to examine closely the minutes of this (Jesus') trial with all its primitive marks of authenticity; its meticulous . . . hearing of hostile witnesses; we make the startling discovery that these very words ('in three days') which reason asserts *could never have been uttered by Christ,* are precisely the words which according to all the witnesses formed the pith and core of the fatal and historic sentence with which He was charged."[14] (See also Matthew 27:62-63.)

FURTHER STUDY

Who Moved the Stone?, by Frank Morison, especially pages 18-24. The entire book is an outstanding polemic for the historicity of the resurrection.

[14]Frank Morison, *Who Moved the Stone?* (New York: Barnes and Noble), p. 24. Used by permission.

THE RESURRECTION
OF JESUS CHRIST

DAY **2**

*the resurrection
event, II*

Luke 24:13-43

QUESTIONS

1. What misunderstandings did these two men show?_____

_____

_____

What was their attitude toward Jesus and the resurrection?

_____

_____

2. What attitude toward Scripture does Jesus show?_____

_____

_____

What is the significance of "Was it not necessary" in verse 26?

_____

_____

3. What evidence here refutes the following contentions designed to explain away the resurrection?

    a. The disciples had hallu-   _____
    cinatory experiences (that is,

they thought they saw Jesus, but He wasn't real).

_____

b. The disciples wished to see Jesus so much that they imagined the experience.

_____

_____

c. The tomb was not really empty.

_____

_____

d. The disciples stole Jesus' body and made up the resurrection story.

_____

_____

_____

COMMENTS

Some thought provokers for answering question three are:
1. The usual pattern of hallucinations include (a) highly individual experiences, (b) intra-group disagreement as to the nature of the experience, and (c) a stimulus which is misinterpreted (for example, seeing someone and mistaking him for someone else). How is the experience of the men on the road just the opposite?
2. Notice that verse 41 says they "still disbelieved."
3. What is implied in verse 34 about the attitude of almost all of the disciples to the report of Jesus' resurrection?

One of the most striking features of the accounts of the resurrection of Jesus Christ is the restraint with which the story is told. The details of the occurrence flow out in a matter-of-fact way. If the resurrection had, in fact, occurred, we could not expect any more commonplace occurrences; but if the resurrection story were a fabrication, we should almost certainly find more bizarre events in the report of it, as we find in some later accounts of the resurrection when men let their minds run wild with absurd details (for example, the pseudonymous gospel of Peter).

APPLICATION

1. Consider the different emotions, such as sadness and amazement, that the two men going to Emmaus must have felt. Imagine that you are one of the men. How would you respond?

_____

_____

_____

2. What suggestions for studying the Bible are given in verses 25-27? See also Luke 24:44-47. _____

_____

_____

STUDY **E**

THE RESURRECTION
OF JESUS CHRIST

John 20:1-29

DAY **3**

*the resurrection
event, III*

QUESTIONS

1. List the details here that accord with those in Luke's account.

_____

_____

_____

_____

2. List the details that differ from, or add to, Luke's account.
Are there any direct contradictions?_____

_____

_____

_____

_____

3. Why do you think Jesus appeared to Mary first?_____

_____

Why did she fail to recognize Him?_____

_____

4. What evidence here refutes the following contentions designed to explain away the resurrection?

a. The disciples stole the body.

_____

_____

_____

b. The "appearances" of Jesus were hallucinations or visions.

_____

_____

_____

c. The disciples wanted to believe that Jesus had risen.

_____

_____

_____

5. How is Thomas like many modern people?_____

_____

_____

How is he *unlike* many modern unbelievers?_____

_____

_____

COMMENTS

Many theories about Christ's resurrection have been advanced in the two thousand years since He lived on earth. They are designed to explain the alleged resurrection in order that it will not be necessary to acknowledge that Jesus arose from the dead. J. N. D. Anderson discusses these in a small booklet, *The Evidence for the Resurrection.*

Every such theory must account for the two primary evidences for the resurrection: (1) the empty tomb and (2) Jesus' appearance to the disciples. The alternative theories usually adequately account for only one of these facts.

APPLICATION

1. If you should become convinced that Jesus had *not* risen,

how would this affect your faith?_____

_____

_____

2. What, to you, is the most compelling "proof" of the resurrection?_____

_____

_____

FURTHER STUDY
1. *Evidence for the Resurrection,* by J. N. D. Anderson.
2. *Basic Christianity,* chapter 4, pages 52-54. The condition of the grave clothes is of unusual interest. Stott suggests, "A glance at these grave clothes proved the reality, and indicated the nature, of the resurrection. They had been neither touched nor folded nor manipulated by any human being. They were like a discarded chrysalis, from which the butterfly has emerged" (p. 53-54).

THE RESURRECTION OF JESUS CHRIST

Acts 13:26-43

DAY 4

Paul's sermon

QUESTIONS

1. Read quickly through verses 13-25 to get the setting of this passage. To whom is Paul preaching and under what conditions?

_____

_____

2. What does Paul say about the relationship of the Jews to the prophets of the Old Testament and to the death of Jesus?

_____

_____

_____

3. What does Paul say are the results of the resurrection?

_____

_____

What warning does he give?_____

_____

4. How does Paul demonstrate the fact of the resurrection?

What use does he make of the Old Testament? Compare this with Jesus' thinking in Luke 24:45._____

_____

_____

_____

COMMENTS

Evidence which confirms the truth of Christianity is most clearly and objectively found in the resurrection of Jesus Christ. J. B. Phillips says, "The resurrection of Jesus is plainly the crux of the Christian faith."[15] For those who are investigating Christianity, it is the "crowning proof" of the truth of Christianity. *Proof* of the resurrection in the mathematical sense is impossible, but the objective historical details are recorded and are available for any who care to look at them. The final *proof* for the individual, however, stems from a conviction that Jesus Christ *was* who He said he was and that He *did* what He said He did.

The early Christians were well aware of the apologetic value of the resurrection. Paul said that Jesus was "declared to be the Son of God . . . by the resurrection from the dead" (Romans 1:4). Peter, in his first sermon, called on the people to see that Jesus was from God by the fact that "God raised him up, having loosed the pangs of death, because it was not possible for him to be held by it" (Acts 2:24). The center of the apostles' message was Jesus Christ, and the most important event in His life was His resurrection.

APPLICATION

1. In communicating our faith to others, how can we follow the apostles' examples? Note that in his message, Paul emphasized a living Person, not merely religious ideas or a code of ethics.

_____

_____

[15]Phillips, *God Our Contemporary,* p. 87. Used by permission.

2. What place does the resurrection occupy in your witness?

_____

_____

What place *could* it occupy?_____

_____

_____

FURTHER STUDY

1. Read the other sermons preached in Acts: 2:14-36, 3:12-26, 5:29-32, 10:34-43. Note the emphasis on the resurrection. How do the apostles demonstrate the fact of the resurrection? What meanings are attached to the resurrection?

2. *Defence of the Gospel in the New Testament,* by F. F. Bruce.

STUDY **E**
THE RESURRECTION OF JESUS CHRIST

I Corinthians 15:1-19

DAY **5**

the significance of the resurrection

QUESTIONS

1. For the past four days we have been considering the facts of Jesus' resurrection; now we need to consider its significance. If forgiveness of sin is all that is necessary for the human being and our sins are forgiven through Christ's suffering and death, why did Christ rise out of death (see also Romans 4:25)?

_____

_____

_____

2. What is the gospel as given in today's passage?_____

_____

To what do Christians witness? Compare Acts 1:8 and 22, 2:32.

_____

_____

What is the significance of the phrase, "according to the Scriptures"?_____

_____

3. How does a message about a living Person differ from good advice, ethics, or ideas about religion?_____

_____

_____

4. What particular problem concerns Paul in this chapter (see v. 12)?_____

_____

What is his logic?_____

_____

_____

COMMENTS

It appears that some people in Corinth had said that there is to be no actual resurrection of the body. Perhaps this rumor was a reflection of the Greek belief that the body imprisons the spirit and true immortality is the spirit's release from the body. Paul launches an enthusiastic attack against this idea in a series of related propositions:

1. If there is no resurrection for anyone, then Jesus could not have risen.

2. If Jesus is not raised, then our gospel has no content, since the resurrection is the core of the gospel.

3. If the gospel is empty, so is our faith in the gospel.

4. Not only that, but we should be liars, "accusing" God of doing something He really did not do.

5. If Jesus did not come back to life, then His death accomplished nothing for our sins. (Why is this? Again see Romans 4:25.)

6. But, of course, Christ *is* raised, as we have already demonstrated.

Paul was very sensitive to the implications of the false idea that there would be no physical resurrection of human beings in the future, because he saw that this implied that Jesus could not have risen. We thus realize that, among all the religions of the world, Christianity alone depends on the historical occurrence of a single event—Jesus' resurrection. Without the resurrection, there is no Christianity.

APPLICATION

1. What great affirmation does Paul give in verse 10?_____

_____

How is this fact true of you?_____

_____

Is your response to the grace of God the same as Paul's?_____

_____

_____

2. What view of death does the resurrection of Jesus give?

_____

_____

In what ways does this view change your attitude toward death?

_____

_____

How do you think and live in light of this view?_____

_____

_____

3. Have you ever explained to a non-Christian why you believe Jesus came back to physical life?_____

What would you say?_____

_____

_____

_____

FURTHER STUDY

If someone were interested in disproving the truth of Christianity, why should he focus his attacks upon the historicity of the resurrection? Why does Paul stake the truth of the gospel on the fact of Jesus' resurrection (v. 14)?

STUDY **E**

THE RESURRECTION
OF JESUS CHRIST

I Corinthians 15:20-58

DAY **6**

*the meaning
of the resurrection*

QUESTIONS

1. What benefits come to man as a result of Jesus' resurrection?

_____

_____

_____

Explain Paul's reference to Adam in this passage._____

_____

_____

2. In your own words answer the question, "How are the dead raised?"_____

_____

_____

_____

3. How does Paul answer the question, "Will there be any change in our resurrected body from the one we have now?"

_____

_____

What is the protoype for our resurrected body (vv. 45-49)?

4. Summarize the teaching that Paul gives concerning what will happen in the future (vv. 24-28, 51-57)._____

_____

_____

_____

_____

5. What is the significance, for men, of Jesus' resurrection as it concerns the fact of death?_____

_____

_____

_____

COMMENTS

From the discussion of the resurrection of Jesus, Paul moves into an explanation of the resurrection of believers, because the former assures the latter. "So you say there will be a resurrection of the body," the skeptics say. "How is that possible when we know that the body decomposes after it is buried?" Paul counters this argument with illustrations from nature and the Scriptures. New plants sprout from buried seed; in this manner new bodies will be given to believers at the return of Jesus Christ. Just as God could give life to Adam, made of the dust of the earth, so He can give life to those who die believing in Jesus Christ.

We can have the assurance that this will indeed occur, because Jesus Himself rose from the dead. And because He overcame death, death is a defeated enemy. It is not the end of our existence, so we need not fear it. Jesus Christ has won a victory for us over death (vv. 53-57 and Colossians 2:15).

But what is a great comfort to believers ought also to be a warning to unbelievers. Not only does the resurrection of Jesus Christ assure believers of life in heaven; it is also an indication that God will judge unbelievers after their resurrections (Acts 17:31 and Revelation 20:13).

APPLICATION

1. With regard to verse 32, *The New Bible Dictionary* says, "Believers are not men for whom this life is all. Their hope lies elsewhere. This gives them perspective and makes for depth in living."[16] In what ways is this true of you?_____

_____

_____

_____

_____

2. If we are to "bear the image" of Jesus Christ ultimately, what can we be doing now in preparation for this?_____

_____

_____

3. What is the significance of the "therefore" in verse 58?

_____

_____

Why do the commands of verse 58 follow from the teaching of this section?_____

_____

What does it mean for you to "be steadfast"?_____

_____

[16]*The New Bible Dictionary*, J. D. Douglas (Grand Rapids: Eerdmans Publishing Co.), p. 1089.

4. What difference does Jesus' resurrection make to you after this week of study?_____

_____

_____

When you understand the meaning of the resurrection, how does this affect your life? Read also Colossians 3:1-4 and Philippians 3:10._____

_____

_____

FURTHER STUDY

1. Read the article entitled "Resurrection," in *The New Bible Dictionary*.

2. Concerning the return of Christ and the resurrection of believers, compare verses 51-57 with I Thessalonians 4:13-18.

3. What light does the fact of the ultimate sovereignty of God over all creation (vv. 20-28) shed on the problems of evil, suffering and turmoil (political and military, for example) in the world?

APPENDIX

*suggestions
for group
discussion study*

Each member of the discussion group should prepare for the discussion by completing a study each day for the week prior to the meeting. The group will concentrate its discussion on one passage from the material of the week. But the leader should encourage the members to bring in related material from the other sections studied during the week. Thus, a synthesis of the biblical teaching on the topic can be achieved.

WEEK **A**   John 8:31-59

Purpose: to understand what Jesus actually claimed about Himself.

Since this section is long, you may prefer to study only part of it, intensively. However, the unit study can give the students in your group a feeling for the development of the animosity of the Jews toward Jesus as they understand what He was claiming about Himself.

PART ONE: verses 31-38

1. What is the spiritual condition of the people listening to Jesus? What caused these people to believe in Jesus (vv. 27-30)? What did they believe about Jesus?
2. What did Jesus say these people must do to be truly His disciples? What does this statement reveal about the relationship between *doing* and *believing* in the Christian life?

3. What does "continue in my word" mean? In how many different ways can this be specifically expressed?

4. What are the effects of sin on a person? Why did Jesus talk about sin to these people who believed on Him?

5. What was offensive about what Jesus said? How does their offense reveal the real requirements Jesus makes? How might you (rightly) offend someone in witnessing?

6. What is freedom? What freedoms do people usually prize the most? What freedom does Jesus offer?

PART TWO: verses 39-59

At the beginning of the study, have the group list every claim Jesus makes about Himself—His origin, His teaching, His Father, etc. This could be done individually on paper or together on a blackboard. The latter is preferable.

1. What is revealed by the people's reaction to Jesus? (Of what is it symptomatic?) What does Jesus say is characteristic of a real Christian? How do actions reveal your true state?

2. What two claims of these people does Jesus refute? What reasoning does He use in His refutation?

3. What great confidence does Jesus show in verse 46? How does this affect your understanding of His right to forgive sin (compare Day 1)?

4. What does Jesus say about His relationship with the Father?

5. How does the conversation end? Why? Why are the Jews infuriated (cf. John 5:18 (Day 5) to see why the Jews want to kill Jesus)?

6. How would you analyze the course of the conversation from verses 31-59?

WEEK **B** Luke 9:23-27, 57-62; Luke 14:25-35
Purpose: to understand what Jesus expects of His followers.

Luke 9:23-27
1. What three things does Jesus command someone who wants to follow Him to do? Explain each of these commands.
2. What does Jesus say is the advantage of following Him?

3. Does this statement of Jesus' demands reveal that Christianity is a hard course for life? Is it unnatural (consider carefully what *natural* and *unnatural* mean)?

Luke 9:57-62
4. Describe what kinds of contemporary people would be like the three men in this paragraph. (Use your imagination. The leader should give the group time to think.)
5. How can Christians sometimes respond to Jesus in ways like these men did? What things or attitudes can hinder you from whole-heartedly following Jesus?

Luke 14:25-35
6. Why does Jesus use such strong language when He talks to the people about being His disciples?
7. What can you learn from Jesus' example for your witnessing?
8. What does Jesus mean when He says His disciples must "renounce all"?

GENERAL DISCUSSION QUESTION:
9. What is the full meaning of Jesus' frequent command, *Follow me*—as seen in this week's six studies?

WEEK **C**   John 15:1-17
   Purpose: to understand the close relationship between Jesus Christ and Christians.
1. To whom is Jesus speaking in this section? How will this answer help you to understand this section accurately?
2. What does the vine allegory illustrate about the relationship between Jesus and His disciples?
3. What seems to be the theme word of this section? *Abide* occurs ten times; what does it mean? How does it differ from *be*? What does it involve? What are the dangers of failing to *abide*? In practical everyday terms what does to abide in Jesus Christ and to have Him abide in you mean?

4. What is said here about *fruit?* What is the meaning of *bearing fruit?*
5. How much of this relationship with Jesus Christ and growth in Christ is the responsibility of God? the responsibility of the individual?
6. What is the meaning of loving one another as Jesus loves? What examples in love has Jesus given (cf. Days 1 and 6)?

WEEK **D**   Isaiah 52:13—53:12
Purpose: to understand the effect of Jesus' death for you.

1. Use the questions in Week 4, Day 5, for discussion.
2. How can you see from this section that Jesus' death was not:
      unexpected,
      accidental,
      involuntary,
      useless,
      ineffective?

GENERAL DISCUSSION QUESTIONS:
3. Observe the parallels between Isaiah 53 and the life and death of Jesus.
4. Refer to the study of Day 6. How do these New Testament sections reflect the teaching of Isaiah 53?

WEEK **E**   I Corinthians 15:1-19
Purpose: to understand the significance of Jesus' resurrection to Christianity.

1. According to Paul in his introductory sentence, what is the subject of his discussion?
2. What does he proceed to discuss?
3. What evidence does Paul list for the fact of Jesus' resurrection? When did these appearances occur?

4. What does Paul say about himself? In what ways is he an example?
5. Why is Paul concerned to establish the fact of Jesus' resurrection?
6. What is the primary meaning of the resurrection?
7. Refer to Question One. What is the gospel Paul preaches? What principles for your witnessing are illustrated?

GENERAL DISCUSSION QUESTIONS:
8. Why do you believe that Jesus actually arose from the tomb?
9. If you should suddenly become convinced that Jesus had *not* risen, what difference would it make to you?
10. What proposals have been made by skeptics to suggest that Jesus did not really rise from death? What do you think of these?

for further study from
InterVarsity Press

GROW YOUR CHRISTIAN LIFE
This book can revolutionize that sagging campus Bible study! How? by offering material for individual study during the week. Then—Wow!—everyone has relevant ideas to share at the group discussion. *Grow Your Christian Life* makes problems such as sin, marriage, fellowship and guidance more lucid and group discussions more meaningful and exciting. And there are 12 weeks of daily studies. 661-8 $1.95

LOOK AT LIFE WITH THE APOSTLE PETER
Jane Hollingsworth and Alice Reid help individuals and groups uncover spiritual treasures from Peter's life and writing. God's work in Peter's life is fascinating. Here are 16 weeks of daily studies from the Gospels, Acts and I Peter. 407-0 $1.25

DISCOVERING THE GOSPEL OF MARK
Jane Hollingsworth helps you discover the teachings in Mark through inductive Bible study principles and gives directions for leading group discussions on Mark. 419-4 $1.25

LEARNING TO BE A MAN
LEARNING TO BE A WOMAN
Kenneth Smith, in these companion volumes, shows what it is to become a man and a woman. These study guides

point you—an individual, a couple, a group—to God and to the Bible. They don't make the learning easy, but they certainly make it possible. And what you learn is yours to keep. *Learning to Be a Man* 692-8 $1.75; *Learning to Be a Woman* 693-6 $1.75

THIS MORNING WITH GOD
Here is a unique daily devotional guide that forces you to study the Bible itself and enables you to experience the joy of independent discovery. Four volumes will take you through the Bible in five years. Vol. 1, 668-5, $1.95; Vol. II, 673-1, $1.95; Vol. III, 674-X, $1.95; Vol. IV, 675-8, $2.50

HOW TO BEGIN AN EVANGELISTIC BIBLE STUDY
Ada Lum tells how Christians can initiate and lead an evangelistic Bible study with their non-Christian friends. 317-1 95¢

JESUS THE RADICAL
Ada Lum focuses on eight studies from the Gospel of John, showing Jesus challenging the capitalists, debating with the Establishment, crashing traditional social barriers. A guide designed especially for evangelistic Bible studies. 316-3 95¢